Contents

Introduction

As the trout fishing public continues to grow in staggering numbers, and as the trophy trout waters become more and more crowded, the pressure on this country's fisheries will increase. What is a flyfisher to do if he or she doesn't want to cast elbow to elbow with twenty other people? Backpack into the high country, of course.

The combination of backpacking and trout fishing gets you to places you might not otherwise visit, some of the prettiest places on earth. Fishing for timberline trout amidst stands of evergreen forests, under craggy peaks, and standing over verdant meadows is what backpack angling is all about. Backpack angling takes you into the Appalachians, the Rockies, the Cascades, the Sierra Nevadas. The trout may not be as big as those found in year-round lowland trout lakes and streams, but they are usually wilder and much prettier. What's more, you won't see many people in these off-the-beaten-path places. Casting away the day under azure skies, away from crowds is indescribably wonderful.

Going into the backcountry doesn't necessarily mean sloshing twenty-five miles through bear-infested forests. Most anglers fish public accesses, like bridges, and don't wander far from these easily accessible spots. However, by being a little more adventurous than your average fisherman, you can find more solitude and get to the less wary trout.

High country fishing has good trout fishing and is almost always on public lands. There is generally good access to trailheads and launch-off points, with many forest service roads, logging and mining roads, trails and trailheads. How far off the road you want to venture is your own choice.

The Backpacking Flyfisher

Mark D. Williams

Illustrations by Susan Newman

Menasha Ridge Press
Birmingham, Alabama

To Sarah Denise; you'll always be daddy's little girl

© 1997 Mark D. Williams
All rights reserved

Printed in the United States of America
Published by Menasha Ridge Press
First edition, first printing

Illustrations by Susan Newman
Text design by Carolina Graphics Group

Note:
Outdoor activities are assumed risk sports. While every effort has been made to insure this book reflects sound techniques, it is only a guide. It cannot be expected to replace appropriate experience and training in fishing or backcountry hiking.

Menasha Ridge Press
700 South 28th Street, Suite 206
Birmingham, Alabama 35243
(800)247-9437
web address: http://www.menasharidge.com

There are thousands and thousands of miles of rarely fished streams teeming with wild and stocked trout. Thousands of high country lakes dot the mountains, and many are fished by only a handful of anglers in a decade.

Most backcountry trout are correctly thought to be rather easy prey (though golden trout are among the most difficult trout I have ever fished). These trout haven't seen many anglers, so they typically are not hardened and finicky. You rarely see mountain trout refusing attractor patterns in favor of smaller, more hatch-specific patterns. However, backcountry trout are wary to any shadows, footfalls, and bad casts. They spend much of their day hiding from raccoons, ospreys, eagles, minks, larger trout and other predators, including bumbling fishermen. So what's to lose? Even if you fail to catch a trout, you'll still be in some beautiful country.

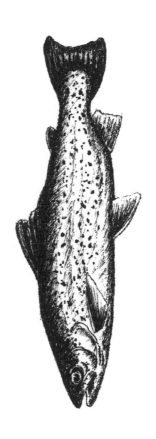

Who This Book is For
The Backpacking Flyfisher is directed to two groups of people: those who backpack but seldom angle for trout, and those who angle for trout but seldom backpack. This book will instruct the reader on what gear to bring (specific to catching trout), as well as outline the strategies for fishing streams and lakes, the kinds of flies to use, and other pertinent information you will need to catch trout in remote places.

Planning Your Trip
Good preparation usually pays off with a more meaningful trip, one in which the scenery and the fishing are worth the hike. There are trout fishing guidebooks for almost all remote regions in the United States as well as numerous backpacking field guides for specific regions across the United States.

You can also plan your own trip by looking at maps, searching for lakes and streams that show some promise. Pull out United States Geological Survey (USGS) topo maps, national forest maps, or county agency maps. Most maps can be useful in putting together a plan of action. The most useful to the backpack angler are the USGS maps, especially the 7.5 and 15 minute maps for the detail they show. I waterproof my maps with a brush-on application available from many backpacking stores.

I look for meadows, places where the creek might have slowed down and the gradient is not as steep. It is in these places that big trout might lurk beneath undercut banks or in beaver ponds. I look for lakes off the main trail, because even backpackers tend to fish the more accessible waters. Headwaters starting at a lake or series of lakes are worth investigating, for trout from the lakes sometimes migrate to and from them. If a trail follows a stream then stops or diverts, this should be a candidate for a backpacking trip. Where a trail ends usually means where other anglers stop as well. Studying a topo map can help alert you to areas where few streams are big enough to bother with or you might locate old logging roads to use as a launching point for your excursion.

You must know how to read a topo map and handle a compass to maneuver in the backcountry and find trout. There are several books in print which cover this territory well. Persons who cannot navigate with a compass have no business hiking around in the backcountry.

Safety
When hiking in the high country, you will encounter a number of hazards. Some of these include: lightning, blisters, bears, snakes, insects, storms, wading, sunburn and exposure to UV rays, getting lost, cold and hypothermia, crime, rac-

coons, falling and breaking a bone or busting your head, altitude sickness, and hooks. Preparation and common sense will keep you from falling prey to most of these dangers, but because nature is so powerful, it is a good idea to backpack with a buddy. These hazards and how to avoid them are extensively covered in many backpacking books.

PACKING

Backpacking Equipment

So what basics should you make sure to pack? What you carry will be your home away from home, but you don't want to take everything (including the kitchen sink). For more in-depth information, you should read a good primer on backpacking, such as Victoria Logue's *Backpacking in the 90s*, published by Menasha Ridge Press, but the following will get you started.

Clothes

What you wear depends a lot on the weather. For warmer weather, I bring along a comfortable pair of pants, a pair with a lot of pockets (to hold chapstick, licenses, etc.), plenty of leg room (to prevent chafing), and these pants also have zip-off legs which turn the pants into shorts. This way, if it gets too hot, I am already wearing my shorts.

Take along plastic bags to place wet clothes in to keep everything else dry.

I wear my fishing shirt, so I bring only one extra shirt. My backpacking clothes tend to be earth colors, because I don't want to take any chances that bright colors scare trout. This controversy has never been proven one way or another, but why take chances?

I recommend packing warm clothes on almost any trip, for just about any place in the country can experience a nasty bout of frigid weather, even in the dead of summer. Definitely bring warm clothes if you plan to hike in higher elevations. Also pack rain gear. In most mountain country, rain is an everyday occurrence. If you are wet, you'll soon be miserable and cold. For this reason, many backpackers choose to wear synthetic materials instead of cotton. Synthetics insulate better than cotton (which is worthless against the cold when wet) and they are much lighter. They do cost more, but in the long run are worth it. Many old hands still prefer wool, which does retain heat when wet, but I see fewer and fewer anglers still wearing wool. I do swear by my wool gloves when fishing cold water.

Regardless of the season or locale, I always carry a pair of warm gloves, a skull cap, a hat to fend off rain and sun, a Polarfleece pullover, a rain poncho and rain pants. I have no time to be freezing cold when I could be fishing. I also wear wick-dry socks that dry quickly, and tuck one pair into my pack.

Layer your clothes to regulate your body temperature. Layering allows you to carry fewer garments. As the day (or you) warms up, shed one or more layer of clothes. As things cool down, put more on.

Waders and Boots

Most of the streams you'll fish won't require wading, and, I dare say, require that you not wade or you'll spook every trout in the river. You generally don't have to ford many streams, and when you do, they are typically narrow and shallow. This being said, I still usually bring some kind of wading shoes because: 1) some of the streams you'll ford are awfully cold; 2) the better trout lie is always on the other side of the stream.

Some anglers use lightweight, stocking-foot nylon waders. These roll up and don't take much space. A disadvantage is that they aren't very durable, and could tear easily, since you'll likely be walking through brush and crawling on your knees to approach spooky trout. The lightweight neoprene waders don't roll up quite as tightly, but they are more durable and comfortable against the cold. If you like the convenience of these waders, it's a good idea to pack a repair kit (duct tape works to fix waders in a pinch).

If waders aren't your style, or you want to keep your pack weight down, try old tennis shoes to splash in the crystal-clear streams. Many glue felt to the soles. Tennis shoes can be strapped onto the outside of the backpack. Disadvantages are that they get heavy when wet and do not provide any ankle support.

Another alternative is the felt-soled sandal offered in most mail-order sporting goods catalogs. These are cheap, light, and don't hold water. But they do leave toes and ankles open to sharp rocks, and they provide no ankle support whatsoever. To keep the tootsies warm, buy neoprene socks to wear under the sandals. If you keep your toes warm, you'll hardly notice the numbing cold on your calves and knees. These socks also come in handy if you choose to ford a stream in your hiking boots.

Whatever wading shoes or boots you wear in the backcountry, I highly suggest felt soles if you plan on wading rocky streams. Felt-soled bottoms won't last long if you wear them on the trail, but replacement felt is inexpensive and easy to glue on (even for a ten-thumbs like me).

Sunglasses

I always wear polarized sunglasses for two reasons: the polarization cuts through the glare and helps me see underwater, and wearing eye protection makes it tougher for a wayward backcast to hook my eye. I consider my sunglasses to be as important to catching trout as my rod, reel or flies. I also suggest you bring along Croakies or eyeglasses lanyards. These will help you keep up with your glasses if you take them off, or keep them on if the wind is gusting, as it often does in higher elevations.

Flashlight

Many times I have stayed on the water past dark, fishing to rising trout I could not see. Having a small flashlight allowed me to tie on new flies without spooking the fish and also lit the way back to camp after staying out late. Anglers can choose between conventional flashlights, or the newer, neater models made for anglers and backpackers which hang around your neck, clip to your cap, or wrap around your head.

Other Equipment

I always carry a survival kit and a first aid kit (see Bob Newman's *Common Sense Survival For Outdoor Enthusiasts*, Menasha Ridge Press). I also carry a lighter, Aqua-pot tablets (and sometimes my water purifier), a knife, a good compass, a camera, and film. I also carry a two-person tent that weighs about five pounds (you can sleep under the stars, but I like knowing I can stay dry in wet weather), a lightweight sleeping bag, and a foam pad. These last two things I strap onto the frame of my backpack. Finally, I bring along food I don't plan on catching and a camp stove to cook it on.

Fishing Equipment

This is the reason you're going out there, right? So you need to be as judicious about what fishing equipment you bring as you are with the backpacking items. I always inspect my gear before packing. I look for nicks and cuts in my flyline. I check the reel to make sure it functions smoothly. I give the rods the once-over to ensure guides are unbroken and smooth, and that the blank has no cracks. Here's what you should think about:

Rods

What kind of rod should you bring? Notice I didn't say "rods." There is no need to haul around a closetful of rods just because backcountry fishing has slightly different outfit requirements. No one rod is going to fit every situation, but in general, a longer rod—an 8- to 9-foot rod in a 4 or 5 weight, either a two-piece or multipiece — will cover most conditions. I like the extra length a 8 1/2- or 9-foot rod gives me, since so much of backcountry stream fishing involves dapping the fly while hiding behind brush or trees. A longer rod gives you better line control, longer reach, and is better for nymph fishing. A longer rod also roll casts easier and loads well.

For fishing most high lakes, a nine-foot, 6 weight rod is the best outfit. Though a shorter 4, 5, or 6 weight travel rod will work fine, a longer rod is better for the longer casts sometimes required when angling on remote lakes. A longer rod loads well and is best for taking line off the water, especially when casting from a float tube.

Some flyfishers use travel rods, which come in three or more pieces for compact packing. They used to feel like casting with a CB antenna, but they have come a long way since then. They are no longer whippy and no longer turn at the ferrules. Also, the manufacturers have managed to impart touch and softer action to these put-together rods. Travel rods pack down to less than thirty-two inches in most cases, fit in protective rod tubes, and are perfect for carrying on planes and strapping onto your backpack.

But don't get pigeon-holed into bringing the latest, four-piece, seven-foot, 3-weight, space-age material pack rod if buying one doesn't fit your budget or your style. To be sure, a travel rod that packs down to twenty-seven inches has its place for many backpacking anglers, but just as many prefer a two-piece that fits into a fifty-inch rod tube, which can be used as a walking or wading staff.

What about a short or light rod? Many anglers swear by their shorter rods (six-and-a-half to seven feet), and some have gone to the lightweight rods of 3, 2, and even 1 weight. A shorter rod is great for tight loops and casting into impossible lies. If conditions are windy or you need to cast big, bushy flies, a heavier line can be loaded on. In many cases, they cast better with the heavier line. However, unless you are a superb caster, you'd be better off avoiding these rods. But if a shorter, smaller rod fits your needs and feels comfortable, you'll fish better.

Flylines

As for flylines, this is again a matter of personal choice. A 4, 5, or 6 weight line, either double taper or weight forward, will cover most conditions on backcountry lakes and streams. A double taper line is useful because fishing rocky streams eventually wears down the end of the flyline, and you can reverse the line on the reel when this happens. The extra distance one gets with a weight forward line is useful for lake flyfishing, but this benefit is often negated on the small streams.

Try a few flylines at your local flyshop, and see what feels best to you. You might try a heavier line on your rod, too—you might like it and it gives you versatility in fighting windy conditions. I recommend looking into sink tip lines if you plan on angling for trout in lakes. One way to economize on gear is to purchase a cassette reel and bring both a floating line and a floating line with a sinktip, or a full sinking line if you will be float tubing.

REELS

Reels are not as important in the backcountry since you will probably not go into the backing very often (though I hope you do). What you do want in a reel is dependability. Nothing ruins a trip quicker than a jammed or broken reel.

There are a number of lightweight, serviceable, inexpensive models on the market today. A single-action reel is all you will need. I would spend a little extra money to get a mid-priced model that doesn't have plastic inner works, but don't blow your entire budget on a reel that stands a good chance of getting banged around in the backcountry.

FLIES

Most anglers have at least 5 or 6 flyboxes, each strategically arranged by color, size, species, pattern or philosophy. The high country streams and lakes require a lot less thought about fly patterns than lower elevation trophy trout streams. A few basic patterns in a few basic sizes is all you'll need most of the time. Not having to dig through zillions of flies and several flyboxes makes flyfishing in the far reaches of the the mountains refreshing. Keep it simple. Sometimes simplicity improves presentation, and I'll take perfect presentation over an exact hatch match anyday.

On the next two pages is a cross-section of the most effective fly patterns for backpacking anglers. This selection includes all the basic and best flies for fishing the backcountry as well as high country lakes. I often carry these flies, and a few more, when I leave the trailhead for upstream fishing. They easily fit into one or two flyboxes. Talk with your local flyshop, or ones near the areas

WETS, EMERGERS, STREAMERS, AND NYMPHS

Hare's Ear (12-18)

Pheasant Tail (12-16)

Prince Nymph (12-16)

Caddis Pupa (12-22)

Comparadun (14-20)

Emergers (Pheasant Tail,
    Baetis, Caddis) (10-18)

Sparkle Dun (14-18)

Surface emergers (Sulphur,
    Rusty Brown, Adult
    Damselfly (10-12)

RS2 Baetis (14-20)

Adult Dragonfly (10-12)

Dragonfly nymph (10-12)

Spinners (16-22)

Damselfly nymph (10-12)

Chironomid (16-22)

Midge Larva & Pupa (16-22)

Scud (16-20)

Stonefly nymphs (brown,
    black, golden, maybe even
    yellow) (4-10)

Timberline Girdle Bug (10-14)

Shrimp (10-18)

Partridge & Green/Partridge
    & Orange (10-14)

Zonker (2-6)

Muddler Minnow (2-8)

Dark Spruce (2-8)

Light Spruce (2-8)

Woolly Buggers (4-12)

Woolly Worm (brown, black)
    (6-12)

Leech (6-10)

Hornberg (6-10)

you plan to fish, for advice on fly choices.

Trout in the remote backcountry respond to any number of well-presented flies. If you like to fish with a particular pattern and have good success with it, bring several sizes. Make sure your selection includes attractor patterns for imitating both mayflies and caddisflies (a few Royal Wulffs and Elk Hair Caddis would do the trick). I would always bring along a handful of ant, beetle, and grasshopper patterns.

For those finicky fish in still pools, beaver ponds, and backwater, I include the best searching pattern ever invented—the Adams, although I prefer an Adams Parachute variation for the visibility of the white tuft. Also include a few streamers and nymphs for those instances when topwater prospecting isn't working.

Flyboxes

Anglers have individual preferences for every piece of equipment, flyboxes included. I never have been able to convince myself I can afford to purchase a Wheatley-type box, the fancy, aluminum kind with all the little window compartments. I use plastic foam boxes for my normal flyfishing trips, but when backpacking, I shrink my fly collection down to fit into a couple of clear plastic, hinged boxes with large compartments. I pack all my dry flies, and some of my nymphs and wets into one plastic box, and all the other bigger streamers and nymphs into another. Other choices for the angler include magnetic boxes which pin down your flies, and the new system-style foam wallets which have interchangeable pads.

Other Fishing Gear

REPAIR KIT: My field repair kit, which I keep in a small army surplus pouch, includes: a small roll of duct tape, Super Glue, a couple of spare rod guides, a spool of rodbuilder's thread, sandpaper,

paper clips, a multi-use tool like the Leatherman tool (which has a screwdriver, a punch, pliers), and reel oil. I also carry an extra rod tip I bought for $12. I have used it only once, and felt justified for all the times I carried it unused.

Rod guides can be temporarily attached in the field with duct tape, or if you are willing to wait fifteen minutes, with Super Glue. If you don't have spare rod guides, a paper clip can be fashioned to work. If your rod shows a crack, wrap it in rod-building thread and apply adhesive. This splint strengthens the weakened area. Check your reel every so often to make sure dirt, sand, or rocks haven't made their way into the housing. A dab of reel oil helps keep the reel parts moving smoothly.

Always carry a field repair kit and keep it on your person. Don't leave it in the backpack back in camp. Nothing ruins the day quite like being on a hatch, catching some whoppers, then getting your rod tip caught in a tree and snapping it off.

SUNDRIES: Other things you'll need: tippet, leaders, floatant, leader sink, weights, nippers, forceps, and a retractor.

I carry leaders in 4X, 5X and 6X. These sizes provide me with coverage for almost all conditions, even for casting tiny flies on mirror-like lake surfaces to finicky golden trout. Many friends of mine take a nearly invisible 7X tippet. I have never found it necessary, but a spool of it weighs only ounces, so bring it if you like it.

The streams in the backcountry tend to run quick and foamy, and will sink even a well-dressed fly, so floatant is a must. There are quite a number of floatants on the market, from pastes to sprays to liquid gel. I can't tell much difference from one brand of floatant to another, but that's a matter of personal preference. The same goes for leader sink.

Anglers will need to bring weights of some sort. Most common is the multi-compartment dis-

DRY FLIES

Griffith's Gnat (12-16)

Elk Hair Caddis (Tan, Black, Olive) (10-16)

Adams (10-18)

Goddard Caddis (12-16)

Adams Parachute (10-18)

March Brown (12-16)

Humpy (10-16)

Dark Hendrickson (12-16)

Irresistible (10-14)

Yellow Humpy (12-16)

H & L Variant (10-14)

Royal Wulff (10-18)

Tan Gulper (14-16)

Renegade (10-16)

Thorax (Sulfur, Tan) (14-18)

Stimulator (Orange, Yellow, Olive) (8-14)

Blue Winged Olive (14-20)

Rio Grande Trude (10-16)

Pale Evening Dun (16-20)

Red Quill (14-18)

Trico/Midge (16-22)

Lt. Cahill (14-18)

Cricket (8-12)

Beetle (6-12)

Black Ant (10-14)

Red Ant (12-14)

Flying Ant (12-14)

Jassid (14-16)

Hopper (4-12)

Mr. Rapidan (for Appalachian waters) (12-16)

Water Beetle (12-16)

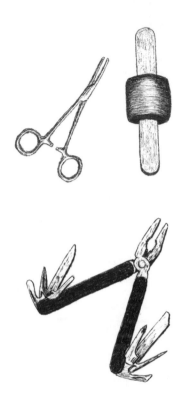

penser with lead microshots of various weight and size. I highly recommend buying non-toxic shot, as this will help keep toxic lead out of our waters. Other weight options include twist-on, malleable weights which come in matchbook form, non-toxic putty that hardens when it meets water, and flat strip lead in spool form.

Nippers, forceps, and retractors are disposable accessories every flyfisher replaces every year or two, not because the products were disappointing but because they were simply lost. Sure, retractors do have an annoying habit of stretching out over time, but I never keep mine pinned on my vest or shirt long enough to worry about that defect. They fall off or get caught on branches.

A friend of mine pins his retractor to the inside of his vest, with the nippers and forceps clipped to the retractor, and then sews it tight. He has yet to lose his retractor, but he buys as many nippers and forceps as I do. You will need nippers for convenience. Don't bite tippet with your teeth—this is tough on the enamel. Use a knife, or combination forceps/scissors, or the elusive nippers. Nippers are also handy because some come with a retractable point to poke through the eye of a fly to clean it, or to help undo tangles.

A neck lanyard is one excellent way to carry many of these fishing goodies. Several types are made specifically for fishermen and are readily available from sporting goods stores or fishing tackle mail order catalogs. You can even make your own. Having a lanyard around your neck with all the whatnots is convenient, takes up little pack space, and if you lose the lanyard, they are cheap to replace.

EVEN MORE SUPPLIES: There are a few last things you might consider, such as nets, strike indicators, flip focal clip-ons, thermometer, hook sharpener, creel, pocketknife or multi-use tool, knot-tier. These are personal items. Take them if you want.

I like a thermometer to test water temperature. Trout feed better in temperatures of 52 to 65 degrees, so it helps to check now and again. I rarely take a net, simply because the trout in streams are not that big. I do carry a net when I float tube, because some of the trout in lakes grow large, but even then I could land them without a net. A net can easily be strapped to the outside of your backpack. If you do take a net, don't bring along one of those big-mouthed jobs. Manufacturers make smaller wooden nets, and one of the newest types of nets is collapsible and fits into a holster or even your shirt pocket.

And what about a float tube? Make sure you can carry the extra weight, you don't have far to travel, and that you really need to use a float tube. Many remote lakes don't require a belly boat.

Choosing Your Backpack

You have to have something to carry all your stuff in. Selecting the proper backpack for your purposes is challenging because of the bewildering array of sizes and styles on the market today—daypacks, rucksacks, external or internal frame backpacks, and fanny packs. Whichever style you choose, get the best one your budget will allow. A backpack is not something to be chintzy about.

I choose to wear an external frame backpack because I can strap and lash so many fishing goodies to the frame, like my wading boots and rod. I also sweat a lot when I hike and the external pack offers much better ventilation. Internal frame packs hold (and compress) an amazing amount of gear and tend not to get caught on branches as you pass through rough terrain. You will find there are tradeoffs to both.

Do your research. Read magazines and books for details on what bells and whistles each style offers. Many backpacks, both internal and external frame, now have sleeves expressly for the purpose of holding a fly-rod travel tube. Try several styles on at your local store before buying. Load the pack to get a sense of how it rides. One word of warning: if you are new to the backpacking gig, don't buy the biggest pack on the market. Stick to a basic style that has about 3,000 cubic inches volume. If you buy bigger, you'll be tempted to fill it.

Other Ways To Carry Gear

If you have a base camp or are just out for the day, you will want something smaller than a backpack to carry your gear.

Fanny packs and chest packs have been improved in recent years. A good fanny pack will hold a bottle or two of water, two flyboxes, a snack, camera, sunglasses, tippet, snippers, and other essentials. Manufacturers now make fanny packs with padding and support, and the cost for a serviceable model is less than fifty dollars. Chest packs aren't as versatile. They only hold your basic fishing stuff, but they are handy and don't weigh much. Chest packs can also be strapped to the outside of your pack.

Daypacks are another good option. Choosing one from varying sizes and weights is a matter of personal comfort. An advantage to daypacks over fannypacks is that a daypack is big enough to carry a rain jacket or sweater. However, don't be tempted to fill it with everything you painfully took the time to include in your backpack.

Some backpacking anglers carry an assortment of carefully chosen goodies in the daypack, like coffeepots, whiskey flasks, extra reel spools, and even waders. Until you know your limits, keep the weight to a minimum. The daypack can also carry a chest pack to your ultimate destination, then hang on a tree limb near the stream or lake.

Don't pack your vest. Vests have too much room. You'll invariably end up stuffing things in the pockets you won't ever use, and in the end, your vest will weigh several pounds and take up a lot of room in your pack. An alternative is to wear a big-pocketed shirt. I own a ratty one, with four bellows pockets, and it has grown faded and worn with time. My wife hates it. I love it. I can stuff two flyboxes into one big pocket, a sandwich into another, floatant and splitshot into yet another, and in the last one, I sometimes stick a candy bar (to which the dark stain will attest).

Think Light!

Backpackers are known for zany weight-saving ideas such as cutting a toothbrush in two, or sawing a bar of soap in half. I pour shampoo into a small vial rather than take a larger bottle, but I draw the line at brushing my teeth with a nubbin of a toothbrush. Also, if one undershirt will do, there is no need to pack two, just in case. Wash out the shirt in the stream, or wear it dirty.

Take the essentials—a heavy pack can quickly tire you out

Sit down and list everything you think you will need. I always lay my stuff out, sort through things I didn't use on the last trip, and discard them. Over the years, I have learned it is better to wash socks on the trail than carry three extra pair in my pack. I now wear pants with zip-off legs, so I don't bring shorts. I stuff all my things into large Ziploc bags, in case the rain gets in my pack.

Before you take your first extended trip, I suggest trying some day trips. Then move up to overnight trips before you rush out to pack forty-five pound packs twenty miles into the wilderness. This will help you learn what stuff is necessary and what isn't. Pare down what you take, and you'll enjoy the simplicity and virtual weightlessness. It is fun to hop from rock to rock like I used to as a kid with a cane pole and a can of worms, and not be weighed down.

To travel light is the rule, but I make exceptions, as you will, for personal things. I like to write in a fishing journal on trips, so I trade off the notebook for something like camp slippers, a luxury many of my fishing buddies enjoy. If you take a lightweight skillet, a book, or a camp chair, try to find something to leave behind. Carrying a heavy pack, when you'd rather be rock-hopping a stream, tires you out and can ruin the trip. You will find a balance after a few trips into the backcountry.

PREPARING TO FISH

You've picked out where you want to fish, and you're all packed, ready to go. What do you do once you get there? There are two basic approaches to fishing the back country. You can park at a trailhead or have someone drop you off, fish, then return to the car or a pre-arranged rendezvous point. Everything you need you carry with you.

The second way is to set up a base camp near a stream, lake, or trail, and take daytrips from the base. Not having to set up camp every evening means less work and more fishing. It also means you can fish a variety of waters, giving you a better chance to land more and bigger trout.

Backcountry Streams

I love to fish small mountain streams. They are all comfortably similar. Most are fast-flowing, cold, clear, and narrow streams typified by pool-riffle configurations, full of smallish but eager wild trout ready to rush to the surface to take a bushy dry fly. In the lower elevations are the meadow streams and spring creeks, the beaver ponds-habitat where anglers will catch the larger trout. You might catch a brown trout at this level to go along with the rainbow trout. There are often cottonwoods lining the bank, and the water moves slowly in places, sliding off into long still pools, back eddies and side channels. At this elevation, backpackers still walk footpaths worn by the occasional anglers who have walked the two or three miles upstream from the main stem of the river. Insect hatches are often thick, and terrestrials, like grasshoppers, are plentiful in the tall grass along the bank.

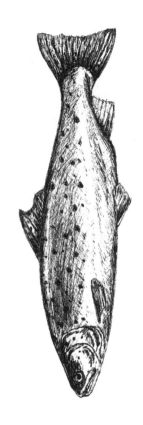

As you move higher, you can fish the rushing water of a canyon section of the same stream, dapping dry flies into pocketwater. Footpaths are harder to find, the pools are shorter, not as deep, and the stream should probably now be called a creek, maybe a brook. In the Appalachians, this part of the stream often becomes a tunnel, canopied by rhododendron and mountain laurel. In the Rockies, this brook runs over more rock, has a faster gradient, and in many sections will have just as many streamside obstacles as the eastern mountain streams. Spruce and aspen stands watch over the creek.

Casts have to be shorter, more idiosyncratic. You will often have to backhand sidearm cast to put the fly under overhanging brush. Each stretch of water puts different demands on your skills, and there will be few places to cast out forty feet of fly-line. You can cast to the edgewater of the long riffles, beside fallen logs, into the tail of a medium-depth pool. There are no brown trout up this far; the water is too cold, the nutrients lacking. Rainbow trout are mixed evenly with brook trout, maybe cutthroats.

Continuing upstream, the creek grows narrower and shallower. Possibly you pass a waterfall or two. The brook tumbles rapidly over a cobble bottom—you are close to its headwaters. You walk beside the timberline, the cold wind whips across the barren ridges, and the clouds move quickly across the sky. The fish are small by any standard, but the short growing season means these trout, almost all of them brook trout, are hungry and eager to rise to almost any well-placed fly—use small, bushy attractor patterns to entice strikes. However, these trout are easily spooked and you often have to crawl just to dap the fly on the water.

Seasonal Variations: Fishing backcountry streams varies from season to season as well as from elevation to elevation. Spring, the beginning of fishing season, comes to the mountains at different times in different places. Some mountain streams open up as early as April, while others lie dormant until July—all high country streams share seasonal variations. Remote streams in lower elevations will be fishable as much as six months of the year while many of the higher altitude waters are fishable less than three months of the year.

During the spring, the volume of water may be unfishable due to heavy rains or snow melt; move upstream where it should become more manageable. Another trick is to hike up feeder streams entering the stream you're currently fishing. You'll be pleasantly surprised by the difference in volume and the increased number of trout lies. During this time, trout will move into eddies or backwater, hug the stream bottom or lurk behind boulders—wherever the current flows slowly. Insects emerge, but imitating them with dry flies is usually fruitless. Nymphing is the only way to fish the high water of spring. Make sure the water temperature is at least forty degrees or you are probably wasting your time.

By summer, the creek's flow has receded to normal levels, and the trout are ravenous. This is dry fly heaven, and for the balance of summer, dry fly fishing is at its peak. The water is still cold, but the heat of a summer day spurs insect hatches and causes trout to look to the top for food. The warmer temperatures of late summer water may drive the trout from many of their lies.

By fall, the water has receded even more, and the resultant low water makes the trout wary. The insects are also smaller; where you fished a size 12 dry fly in the spring, a size 14 during the summer, you will now have to drop down to a size 16. Oxygenated water is at a premium and the slow, shallow water does not provide enough oxygen. The trout cannot hold in the deep pools for lack of oxygen, so they move into the oxygen-rich riffles, or swim upstream to cooler water. Look for spring-fed holes, long riffles, and foamy pocket water to find trout. Brook and brown trout are spawning, rich in color, and aggressive in feeding habits. Fish inlets and outlets to lakes, and feeder creeks to bigger rivers, for spawning fish will swim upstream in search of appropriate spawning ground.

Insects and Flypatterns

The water in these streams is fast, clear, and cold; nutrients are rushed away as the stream tumbles down the rocky slopes. Insects are fewer, as they cannot tolerate the water temperature, the short season, and the lack of egg-laying habitat. The main insects the trout feed upon are mayflies, caddisflies, stoneflies, midges, and terrestrials. Forage fish are scarce at these higher elevations.

To imitate these insects, you won't need lessons in taxonomy or Latin. For the high country, attractor patterns which ride high on the fast water work best. Many backpackers fish nothing but dry flies on small streams. The relative shallowness of the water, combined with the aggressiveness of the opportunistic trout, means they can be holding on the bottom of the stream and will still rush to the surface to take a passing fly.

One of the keys to catching fish in remote streams is to fish with flies that are visible to you, the angler. If you can see the fly, a fluffy, bright pattern, like a Royal Wulff, then you can watch as it bounces over riffles and through foamy pocket water. And if you can see the fly, then you can watch for fish striking. This means you will catch more fish. It often is difficult to fish the more precise patterns, such as a Red Quill or Blue Winged Olive, because these slimmer, lighter-dressed patterns tend to get lost in the action of the current.

Strategies and Tips

If you come away with only one piece of advice about trout fishing the high country from this book, take this: keep your fly on the water. Don't waste time false casting. Don't worry about style or grace. You're out to catch fish, and fish don't fly. Keep your fly on the water.

Take your time approaching the water lest you spook the trout

Footfalls on the bank are anathema to hooking up with these high country trout. Walking heavily on the stream is the surest way to cause wild trout to flee for cover. Trout will also refuse the best-placed fly if they have spotted you or your shadow. Learn to stay low and back away from the stream. When hiking from one good section to the next, I often walk three or four feet from the bank, walking softly, and keeping my fly on the water. Sneak up to the stream and hide behind trees and bushes. If cover is unavailable, then you must stay low, shuffling on bended knees, at times even crawling up to the bank. That's much of the fun of fishing these pristine waters—the stalking, the stealth, the hunt.

I practice a dapping technique, too, one of the best for these small streams. Reel in most of your line, leaving only about two to three feet of leader hanging from the rod. Hold the rod over the water, keep the line taut, and let it go with the flow. Dance the fly on the water, or skate it across. Skating a caddis imitation also imitates the way these insects flutter on the water. The technique is especially effective against undercut banks. Dapping allows you to reach these near banks when you couldn't otherwise.

The worst mistake you can make is to be in a hurry. You have hiked all this way, you're tired of carrying the backpack, and the stream is beautiful and inviting. So you tie on any old fly, rush up to the water's edge, and cast across the stream to the far bank. You have scared off most of the trout in this section of water.

Instead, find a high spot overlooking the stream, sit down, and watch for telltale signs of trout. Look for rising trout. Notice if there are any adult insects flying over the water, landing on the surface. Search for swallows and other birds dipping on the stream picking off egg-laying insects. Inspect streamside branches to see what kind of insects are present. Shake bushes to see what flies out. Kick the grass to see if grasshoppers fly out.

One of the best methods for playing trout detective is to turn over underwater rocks. This will give you an idea of the types of insects in the area and their respective stages of development. Sneak up to backwater eddies and simply look at what insects are floating on top. Some anglers use a homemade screen or dip net to trap the various insects in the water.

And finally, look for trout finning in the stream. Look at the shallow water behind a midstream rock, and you'll likely see the dark back of a trout. Feeding trout often show the white of their mouth. Fish feeding off the bottom will show telltale flashes of silver, and it is fairly easy to spot a trout tail rising from the bottom of a pool. It takes some training, and polarized glasses, but you can see fish underwater.

Finding the trout before you cast means you have enough information to make sensible choices. It means you can choose to cast to the largest trout in the pool with an appropriate fly pattern, rather than blindly casting over feeding fish with a fly bigger than any insect in their habitat.

Fish early and late in the day for best results, since this is when fish feed most actively. There are exceptions to every rule, of course. I have had some of my best angling days during sunny afternoons because the cold stream water was warming from the sun. This meant insects were moving about, hatching, and trout were moving about. Midday hatches are usually not as intense as early or late spinner falls, but they help get you through slow periods.

Don't quit fishing if the weather turns overcast or rainy or cold. That is perfect fishing weather. The humidity and rain help keep insects on the water, and trout feeding on them. Rain flushes terrestrials like ants and beetles and inchworms into the stream.

Fish beaver ponds and spring creeks, which usually hold the biggest trout in the stream. Casting on these stillwaters requires your best casts, and catching trout requires mostly luck.

If you do not see an extensive hatch to match, then one of the best ways to prospect for trout is by using a dropper rig. Tie a dry fly to the end of your tippet, preferably an attractor that floats well, like a Royal Wulff or Rio Grande King. To either the eye or the shank of the hook, attach with a clinch knot a piece of tippet from ten to eighteen inches long, depending on how deep the stream.

To this, tie a basic nymph pattern, such as a Hare's Ear or a Prince Nymph. Then pinch on a small splitshot six inches above the bottom fly. If you have looked under some rocks, then you may have seen some cased caddis or other insect larvae to imitate. I usually attach a size 14 beadhead Hare's Ear to the end of this rig. Float the dropper rig in all the likely lies, especially over shallow riffles with a bed of rocks, and the strikes from trout will clue you in to whether they are feeding on top or bottom, and what size and color insects they are eating.

Don't be afraid to experiment. If trout are rising to your flies but refusing, they may be susceptible to passing a floating nymph or an emerger over them. Try to be observant to the stages of the hatch, then choose a fly that approximates that stage. Most of the time, this will require you to cast upstream and float your fly deaddrift, stripping in line. But because of the small size of most backcountry streams, you are often required to modify your casts. You will find yourself sidearm casting and immediately mending line in order to pass your fly under overhanging branches.

Other situations will force you to pile line in front of you and let the fly drift downstream to cover water. When you do fish deaddrift downstream, remember not to strike too quickly when you see the fish take, or you will pull the fly from the trout.

Sometimes, if you will just make your casts shorter, you will hook up with more fish. This often eliminates many of the problems of longer casts. You won't have to mend over so many crosscurrents or line as many fish.

Backcountry Lakes

Backcountry lakes vary from one or two acres in size up to thirty or more acres. Fishing in the lower lakes begins as early as late spring and lasts until late October, early November. At the higher elevations, the season is a few months shorter, and a hard winter can mean only a month or two of productive fishing.

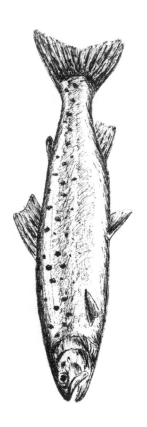

The size and number of trout found in backcountry lakes depends on several factors, among them the size of the lake's littoral zone—the section of a lake warmed by sunlight that enables vegetation and trout food sources to grow. A lake will hold trout only where the sun reaches the bottom. The dark areas of a lake that never receive sunlight are black holes for trout—no aquatic insects, no vegetation, and no trout. Trout prefer the littoral zone not only for the vegetation and insects but also because the water is warmer. They cruise in search of food, because unlike trout living in streams, food doesn't come to them.

At lower elevations, backcountry lakes can be surprisingly fertile, rich with aquatic weeds and full of freshwater shrimp and baitfish—food sources perfect for large trout. Because high country lakes are higher in elevation, the lakes don't warm up as much, and they have shorter seasons. High country lakes also have little or no surrounding vegetation, so they tend to be less fertile, though there are special conditions which preclude normal conditions, producing trout as big as five or six pounds.

An alpine lake is a special type of high country lake that has been carved out by ancient glaciers, which in their retreat, scraped out bowls that filled with water. Most of these were barren of trout until man stocked them in the last century. Alpine lakes have consistent configurations. At one end of the lake, a cliff overlooks the clear, blue-green water; this cirque reflects the deepest end of the the lake; it is unlikely you will find trout here. Opposite of the cirque is the moraine, the shallowest (and warmest) part of the lake.

Insects and Fly Patterns

Many high country lakes have a diversity of trout food. Your fly patterns will need to reflect this. Midges, mayflies and caddisflies are common to

most remote lakes. Other foods include dragon-
flies, damselflies, scuds, leeches, water beetles,
water fleas, snails, and occasionally, at lower elevation lakes, forage fish.

Leeches, scuds and snails are usually found in
lower elevations, but there are exceptions to the
rule. I have fished with these patterns in lakes
where I knew no scuds existed, and still caught
fish because freshwater shrimp flies look so edible
to the trout. There are a number of patterns to imitate each of these, and I would suggest consulting
a fly shop for patterns specific to the region you
plan to fish.

It is imperative to carry wets, emergers, pupa,
and nymphs to properly cover the stages of insect
development. Most of the patterns are on the
smaller size, but there is something to be said for
sticking a few oversized nymphs into your flybox.
Sometimes, with a size 4 Woolly Bugger or size 6
Bucktail, I have saved an otherwise fishless day by
slow-stripping these big flies across drop-offs and
ledges.

Strategies and Tips

As with fishing streams, don't be in a hurry. Stay
away from the bank until you have watched for
cruising trout. Trout cruise in more or less regular
feeding lanes, sometimes making figure eights,
sometimes circling the lake. Their feeding lanes
vary, but these lanes almost always include water
shallow enough to sight the trout. Figure out how
much time it takes before a trout makes it back to
where you first spotted him. Then you can time
your casts to cross paths with the trout.

Look for the trout's cruising lanes in high-country lakes

Most novices, and many experienced anglers,
make the mistake of wading into the shallows and
casting out to the middle of the lake. What they
have just done is wade through the feeding lanes
of the trout, and have probably terrorized several
dozen trout hanging out in the shallows. If you

carefully fish the shallows first, then you will catch more trout.

As you approach the lake, be as wary as the trout. Lakes have very clear water, so the trout can see you a long way off. False casting is not a no-no, but you do want to temper it. A flash of sunlight off the rod, or the slap of the line on the water is all it takes to put fish down. If you wade, do so gently, slowly, so as not to spook trout.

The still, clear water also means you can spot trout and sight cast to them. When the wind makes the surface choppy or when rain peppers the lake, it becomes tougher to sight cast to trout, but the trout are no longer as wary, and usually become more aggressive feeders, perhaps because they feel safer. If it is windy, fish the leeward side, for the wind will blow over all kinds of terrestrials, spinners, and other insects. Foam lines capture insects, so cast around them, too.

Look for special conditions that might indicate where larger-than-normal trout lurk. A lake might have a solid population of invertebrates, others an excellent population of aquatic beetles, and still others rich feeder streams which furnish the lake's trout with an abundant supply of insects. Some lakes enjoy hidden underground springs which warm the water and increase the length of the growing season. A lake full of scuds (freshwater shrimp) can grow some awfully fat fish.

Always begin fishing around any inlets and outlets. An inlet is a natural funnel for washing loads of insects into the lake. We are talking bugs, bugs, bugs. Work around any structure, such as fallen timber, underwater rocks, drop-offs and ledges, points, shoreline, over aquatic weedbeds, and the edges of both weedbeds and bottom types, like where the lake bottom goes from sandy to rocky. Trout sometimes hold against cliffs. Look for any underwater channels.

Most of the trout you will catch on remote

lakes will be caught with subsurface flies, not dry flies. To be sure, you will encounter on almost any lake you visit, at all times during the day, literally hundreds of dimples on the surface. These are feeding fish, but rings on the lake don't necessarily mean these fish are feeding on the surface. And when they are, most of the time these are the smaller fish in the lake.

Unlike stream fishing where you can turn over rocks to figure out how to match the hatch, lake fishing takes a little more guesswork. Because these trout cannot afford to be selective, you can use their opportunistic nature to your advantage.

I am not convinced that the fly pattern is as important as form or presentation for successful remote lake trout fishing. I sometimes begin with a basic wet fly, like a Royal Coachman or Partridge and Orange, as a prospecting fly. Once I have spotted cruising trout, and have determined their general feeding lanes, I cast ahead to the trout, twitch retrieve in front of the trout, and wait for the inevitable strike.

Of course, the trout do not always strike, but more times than not, if I have not spooked them with a bad cast, the trout will rush to the fly from as much as five feet away. If I can see insects on the water, I try to imitate them, but mostly, fishing for trout underwater requires trial and error in an attempt to find out what these fish are keying on.  This means starting off with basic nymphs, buggy flies, like the Hare's Ear, and stripping it in varying speeds in front of visible trout. You can also do this blindly if the weather is whipping up the water's surface. The idea is not so much to match the hatch, but to locate where fish are hiding.

One of the disappointments of hiking the backcountry is finding out that the lake that fished so well the year before has lost all of its trout population over the winter. All lakes must be deep enough to survive the harsh winter, or the lake will suffer winterkill and be barren. However, remote lakes are worth hiking to because they are seldom fished and hold the opportunity to hook up with the most colorful trout. Additionally, most alpine lakes are systematically stocked every three or four years with rainbow, brook, cutthroat, and occasionally golden trout, as well as grayling.

Float tubing is seldom necessary to fish successfully on high lakes, but there are certain advantages in covering a lot of water that could not be fished otherwise. A float tube allows the angler to fin to the middle of the lake and cast back toward shore where the fish are. It also allows the angler to troll when things are slow. As I say, there are few remote lakes I have to use a float tube to fish, but for many, this creates an advantage over wily trout.

Conclusion

Backpacking into the backcountry can be rewarding, especially if the day is spent flyfishing a remote creek or lake. I encourage catch-and-release fishing to preserve our fragile resources, but taking the occasional trout for dinner seems to me to be logical and in keeping with the spirit of the sportsmanship of fishing. This is a personal choice, and to many, a moral choice. Make sure you only take fish which are in abundance, such as brook or rainbow trout. Since golden trout and bull trout, also known as Dolly Varden, are rare, please take care with them and return them immediately to the water. Carefully handle any fish you plan to release. If snapping pictures, keep the trout in the water until your camera is focused.